Productivity the Lazy Way

How Smartness will always Win Over Long Hours

Robert Lidee

Copyright
All rights reserved. No part of this publication may be reproduced, distributed, or transmitted in any form or by any means, including photocopying, recording, or other electronic or mechanical methods, without the prior written permission of the publisher, except in the case of brief quotations embodied in critical reviews and certain other non-commercial uses permitted by copyright law.

Table of Contents

Introduction 5

Part 1...8

  Chapter 1...9

  The Art of Working Smarter, Not Harder...........................9

    The Myth of Endless Hustle....................................11

    Simplifying your approach to tasks 14

  Chapter 2 17

  Mindset Shifts for Simplified Productivity 17

    Smart Strategies Over Endless Toil 19

    Breaking Free from Busywork 21

    Prioritization techniques.....................................23

  Chapter 3 27

  The Enemy...27

    Multitasking 27

    Distraction..29

    Confusion 31

Part 2 36

Execute 36

  Chapter 4 37

  Focused Action 37

    The Power of Single-Tasking 39

    Deep work... 41

    Overcoming Procrastination 43

    Creating Simple Routines 46

    Prioritizing Essential Tasks...................................50

    Streamlining Decision-Making................................52

Productivity, the Lazy Way -

Chapter 5...57

Time Mastery 57

Time Blocking 58

Efficient Meetings and Communication 61

Collaboration and Delegation... 66

Part 3.. 74

Thrive 74

Chapter 6..75

Living the Productive Habits...75

Cultivating consistency.................................... 78

Building momentum.. 79

Tracking progress 82

Chapter 7.. 87

Balancing Ambition and Well-Being................................ 87

Reflecting on Milestones, Progress and Growth...........90

Chapter 8 95

Harnessing Energy for Productivity and Well-Being........ 95

Building effective teams 99

Nurturing relationships.................................... 102

Chapter 9...105

Self-Care for High Performers...105

Physical Health Essentials.. 108

Thriving in the Face of Challenges 111

Conclusion 115

Introduction

Welcome to the world of productive laziness. In a society that often glorifies hustle culture and the grind, the idea of being productive while maintaining a sense of ease and relaxation might seem counterintuitive. However, this book aims to challenge that notion by introducing you to the concept of lazy productivity - a mindset that prioritizes efficiency, effectiveness, and smart work over the traditional notion of putting in long hours.

In this introductory section, we'll lay the groundwork for understanding what lazy productivity entails and why it's a game-changer in today's fast-paced world.
In Part 1: Simplify, we will explore the multifaceted nature of simplification and its profound impact on productivity and well-being. Through a series of in-depth discussions, case studies, and practical exercises, you will gain a deeper understanding of how simplifying various aspects of your life can lead to greater clarity, focus, and effectiveness.

We will begin by examining the importance of decluttering your physical environment. You'll discover how a tidy workspace can enhance your ability to concentrate, foster creativity, and reduce feelings of overwhelm. We'll provide actionable tips and techniques for organizing your surroundings in a way that promotes productivity and peace of mind.

Next, we'll explore the concept of simplifying your goals and priorities. You'll learn how to identify what truly matters to you and align your actions with your values and aspirations. By cutting through the noise and honing in on your core objectives, you'll be better equipped to make meaningful progress towards your dreams without feeling scattered or overwhelmed.

In addition to simplifying your external environment and goals, we'll also delve into the importance of streamlining your daily routines and habits. You'll discover how small changes in your habits can have a significant impact on your overall productivity and well-being. From optimizing your morning routine to establishing effective time management strategies, you'll learn how to cultivate habits that support your goals and enhance your quality of life.

Throughout this book, we'll emphasize the interconnectedness of simplification and productivity. By embracing simplicity in all areas of your life, you'll free up mental and physical space to focus on what truly matters. Whether you're striving to excel in your career, pursue creative endeavors, or nurture meaningful relationships, simplifying your approach can help you achieve greater success with less effort.

So, get ready to embark on a journey of discovery and transformation as we explore the power of simplification in "Productivity the Lazy Way: How Smartness Wins Over Long Hours." Together, we'll uncover practical strategies for simplifying your life and unlocking your full potential in the most effortless and enjoyable way possible.

Part 1
Simplify

Streamlining Your Path to Productivity

1. Introduction to Lazy Productivity:
   - Embracing efficiency over excessive effort is the cornerstone of lazy productivity.
   - Lazy productivity challenges the notion that endless hustle is the only path to success.

2. Mindset Shifts for Simplified Productivity:
   - Shifting from a culture of overwork to one of strategic prioritization is essential for simplified productivity.
   - Prioritization techniques empower individuals to focus on what truly matters, rather than getting bogged down by busywork.

3. The Enemy (Multitasking, Distraction, Confusion):
   - Multitasking may seem efficient but often leads to decreased productivity and lower-quality outcomes.
   - Confusion arises when tasks lack clarity or priority, hindering progress and causing unnecessary stress.

Chapter 1

The Art of Working Smarter, Not Harder

"The Art of Working Smarter, Not Harder" is a philosophy that resonates deeply in today's fast-paced and demanding world. It's about achieving maximum results with minimum effort, optimizing efficiency, and finding innovative ways to accomplish tasks without burning out. Let's delve into this concept extensively, making it relatable by exploring its principles and practical applications.

1. Embracing Efficiency

Working smarter involves prioritizing tasks based on their importance and urgency. It's about recognizing that not all tasks are created equal and focusing your energy on activities that yield the greatest return on investment. This might mean delegating low-impact tasks, automating repetitive processes, or leveraging technology to streamline workflows.

For example, imagine you're a small business owner juggling multiple responsibilities. Instead of spending hours manually processing invoices, you could invest in accounting software that automates the process, freeing up your time to focus on strategic decision-making and business growth.

2. Leveraging Your Strengths

Working smarter also means playing to your strengths and delegating tasks that fall outside your expertise. It's about recognizing that you don't have to do everything yourself and leveraging the skills and talents of others to achieve collective success.

Consider a team project where each member brings unique strengths to the table. By assigning tasks based on individual strengths and expertise, you can optimize productivity and foster a collaborative environment where everyone thrives.

3. Setting Clear Goals

Working smarter involves setting clear, achievable goals and breaking them down into actionable steps. It's about aligning your efforts with your overarching objectives and regularly evaluating your progress to ensure you're on track.

Think about a fitness journey where your goal is to run a marathon. Instead of aimlessly running every day without a plan, you could follow a structured training program tailored to your fitness level and timeline. By setting specific milestones and tracking your progress, you can work smarter towards reaching your ultimate goal.

4. Continuously Learning and Adapting
Working smarter requires a growth mindset and a willingness to learn and adapt. It's about staying curious, seeking feedback, and embracing failure as an opportunity for growth.

Consider a software developer learning a new programming language. Instead of sticking to familiar tools and techniques, they could invest time in learning new skills and staying abreast of industry trends. By continuously expanding their knowledge and expertise, they can work smarter and stay ahead of the curve in a rapidly evolving field.

In essence, the art of working smarter, not harder, is about adopting a strategic approach to productivity that maximizes efficiency, leverages resources effectively, and prioritizes well-being. By embracing this mindset and incorporating its principles into your daily life, you can achieve greater success and fulfillment with less effort.

The Myth of Endless Hustle

In today's hyper-connected world, the myth of endless hustle pervades our culture, glorifying the idea of perpetual busyness as a badge of honor. We're bombarded with messages that equate success with the number of hours we work, the size of our to-do lists, and our ability to juggle multiple commitments simultaneously. However, beneath the surface lies a dangerous fallacy that perpetuates stress, burnout, and a chronic sense of dissatisfaction.

The myth of endless hustle suggests that the key to success lies in working harder, faster, and longer than everyone else. It portrays sleepless nights, skipped meals, and constant multitasking as necessary sacrifices on the altar of achievement. We're told that if we want to get ahead, we must always be on the go, hustling 24/7, and never slowing down for a moment's rest.

But the reality is far from glamorous. The relentless pursuit of productivity at all costs takes a toll on our physical health, mental well-being, and relationships. We sacrifice precious moments with loved ones, neglect our own needs, and overlook the importance of downtime and self-care. In the quest for success, we often lose sight of what truly matters and find ourselves trapped in a cycle of overwork and exhaustion.

Moreover, the myth of endless hustle perpetuates a culture of comparison and competition, where success is measured by external markers such as status, wealth, and recognition. We're constantly bombarded with images of influencers living seemingly perfect lives, effortlessly juggling careers, families, and hobbies with ease. Yet, behind the façade lies a reality that's far more nuanced and messy.

In truth, success is not defined by how busy we are or how many tasks we can tick off our list in a day. It's about finding a sense of purpose, fulfillment, and balance in our lives. It's about cultivating meaningful connections, pursuing our passions, and nurturing our well-being. It's about recognizing that true productivity is not about doing more but doing better - focusing on what truly matters and letting go of the rest.

Breaking free from the myth of endless hustle requires a shift in mindset - a recognition that our worth is not defined by our productivity or our ability to constantly hustle. It involves setting boundaries, prioritizing self-care, and learning to say no to the endless demands of a busy world. It's about reclaiming our time, energy, and autonomy and embracing a more sustainable and fulfilling approach to work and life.

This myth of endless hustle is a seductive yet dangerous narrative that undermines our well-being and perpetuates a culture of overwork and burnout. By challenging this myth and redefining success on our own terms, we can create a more balanced, fulfilling, and sustainable way of living and working.

Simplifying your approach to tasks

Simplifying your approach to tasks is a fundamental principle of productivity that can lead to more efficient and effective results. Instead of getting caught up in complexity and overwhelm, simplification encourages you to streamline your workflow, focus on essential tasks, and eliminate unnecessary distractions. Let's explore why simplifying your approach to tasks is essential and how you can implement it in your daily life.

1. Clarity and Focus
Simplifying your approach to tasks starts with gaining clarity about your goals and priorities. By clearly defining what needs to be done and why it matters, you can focus your energy and attention on the tasks that will have the most significant impact. This clarity helps you avoid getting bogged down by unimportant details and enables you to make more informed decisions about how to allocate your time and resources.

2. Eliminating Unnecessary Complexity
Complexity is the enemy of productivity. When tasks become overly complicated, it's easy to feel overwhelmed and lose sight of the bigger picture. Simplifying your approach involves breaking tasks down into smaller, more manageable steps and removing any unnecessary complexity or redundancy. This might involve automating repetitive tasks, delegating tasks to others, or using tools and technology to streamline workflows.

3. Time Management

Simplifying your approach to tasks also requires effective time management. Instead of trying to do everything at once, focus on the tasks that are most important and time-sensitive. By concentrating on one task at a time and avoiding multitasking, you can work more efficiently and avoid feeling overwhelmed.

4. Setting Realistic Expectations

Simplifying your approach to tasks also means setting realistic expectations for yourself and others. Recognize that you can't do everything, and it's okay to say no to tasks that don't align with your goals or priorities. Be honest with yourself about what you can realistically accomplish in a given timeframe, and don't be afraid to delegate or ask for help when needed. By setting realistic expectations, you can avoid overcommitting yourself and ensure that you're focusing your energy on tasks that truly matter.

5. Continuous Improvement

Finally, simplifying your approach to tasks is an ongoing process of continuous improvement. Take the time to regularly review your workflows and identify areas where you can further streamline processes or eliminate inefficiencies. Be open to feedback from others and be willing to adapt your approach as needed. By continuously seeking ways to simplify and optimize your workflows, you can maintain peak productivity and

achieve greater success in your personal and professional
endeavors.

In conclusion, simplifying your approach to tasks is
essential for maximizing productivity and achieving your
goals. By gaining clarity, eliminating unnecessary
complexity, prioritizing effectively, setting realistic
expectations, and continuously improving your
workflows, you can work more efficiently and effectively
while reducing stress and overwhelm. So, embrace the
power of simplification and watch as your productivity
soars.

Chapter 2

Mindset Shifts for Simplified Productivity

In the pursuit of simplified productivity, it's crucial to recognize that it's not just about adopting new techniques or strategies; it's also about cultivating the right mindset. Our mindset shapes our beliefs, attitudes, and behaviors, ultimately influencing how we approach tasks and navigate challenges. In this chapter, we'll explore several mindset shifts that can help you embrace simplified productivity and unlock your full potential.

1. Embrace Minimalism
One of the key mindset shifts for simplified productivity is embracing minimalism. Minimalism is about focusing on what truly matters and eliminating the excess - whether it's physical clutter, mental distractions, or unnecessary commitments. By adopting a minimalist mindset, you can streamline your life and create space for what's truly important, leading to greater clarity, focus, and peace of mind.

2. Value Quality Over Quantity
In a world that often equates productivity with the sheer volume of tasks accomplished, it's essential to shift your focus from quantity to quality. Instead of trying to do more, strive to do better. Focus on tasks that align with

your goals and values, and commit to delivering high-quality work rather than spreading yourself thin across numerous projects. By prioritizing quality over quantity, you can achieve greater impact with less effort.

3. Embrace Imperfection

Perfectionism is a common barrier to simplified productivity. The belief that everything must be flawless before it's deemed acceptable can lead to procrastination, anxiety, and paralysis. Instead, embrace imperfection as a natural part of the creative process. Recognize that perfection is unattainable and that striving for it only holds you back. Embrace the concept of "good enough" and focus on making progress rather than seeking perfection in every task.

4. Cultivate a Growth Mindset

A growth mindset is essential for embracing simplified productivity. Instead of viewing challenges as insurmountable obstacles, see them as opportunities for growth and learning. Embrace the idea that your abilities can be developed through dedication and effort, and approach tasks with a sense of curiosity and resilience. By cultivating a growth mindset, you can overcome setbacks more effectively and continue to evolve and improve over time.

Embracing these mindset shifts can help you cultivate a more simplified approach to productivity. By embracing minimalism, valuing quality over quantity, embracing imperfection, cultivating a growth mindset, and practicing mindfulness, you can streamline your life and work more efficiently and effectively. Remember that mindset shifts take time and practice, so be patient with yourself as you integrate these principles into your daily life. With persistence and dedication, you can achieve greater simplicity, clarity, and fulfillment in your pursuit of productivity.

Smart Strategies Over Endless Toil

Embracing smart strategies over endless toil is a message that resonates deeply with many of us, especially in today's fast-paced and demanding world. We live in a society that often glorifies the hustle culture - the idea that success is directly proportional to the amount of time and effort we put into our work. However, this mindset can lead to burnout, stress, and a never-ending cycle of exhaustion.

Imagine this scenario: You're a hardworking professional, dedicated to your career and committed to achieving your goals. You pride yourself on your work ethic and your ability to push through challenges with sheer determination and grit. However, despite your best efforts, you find yourself feeling overwhelmed and depleted, constantly struggling to keep up with the demands of your job and personal life.

This is where the concept of embracing smart strategies over endless toil comes into play. Instead of relying solely on brute force and long hours to get ahead, it's about working smarter, not harder. It's about recognizing that productivity is not just about how much you do, but how effectively you do it.

For example, rather than working late into the night to meet a deadline, you might explore alternative strategies such as breaking the task down into smaller, more manageable steps, delegating certain aspects to colleagues, or leveraging technology to automate repetitive tasks. By adopting a strategic approach, you can achieve the same results in less time and with less effort.

Moreover, embracing smart strategies over endless toil is about prioritizing your well-being and recognizing the importance of balance in your life. It's about setting boundaries, saying no to tasks that don't align with your priorities, and making time for self-care and relaxation.

Think about it this way: Would you rather spend countless hours grinding away at your desk, sacrificing your health and happiness in the process? Or would you prefer to work efficiently and effectively, freeing up time to pursue your passions, spend time with loved ones, and recharge your batteries?

By embracing smart strategies over endless toil, you can achieve greater success and fulfillment in both your professional and personal life. So, the next time you find yourself tempted to work yourself into the ground, remember that there's a smarter way to approach productivity - one that prioritizes efficiency, effectiveness, and well-being.

Breaking Free from Busywork

Breaking free from busywork is a liberating journey that many of us can relate to. Busywork, often disguised as productivity, can consume our time and energy without yielding meaningful results. It's the endless stream of minor tasks, distractions, and trivialities that keep us occupied but don't contribute to our long-term goals or well-being. In this chapter, we'll explore how to identify and break free from busywork, reclaiming our time and focus for what truly matters.

Recognizing Busywork
The first step in breaking free from busywork is recognizing it for what it is. Busywork can take many forms - from excessive email checking and social media scrolling to mindless administrative tasks and unnecessary meetings. It's anything that keeps us busy without moving us closer to our goals or fulfilling our purpose.

Prioritizing Purposeful Work

Once we've identified busywork, the next step is to prioritize purposeful work. This involves clarifying our goals, values, and priorities and aligning our activities with them. Instead of getting caught up in busyness for busyness' sake, we focus on tasks that have a meaningful impact on our lives and the lives of others.

Streamlining Processes

Streamlining processes is another key strategy for breaking free from busywork. This involves identifying inefficiencies in our workflows and finding ways to automate, delegate, or eliminate tasks that don't add value. By streamlining processes, we can free up time and energy for more meaningful activities.

Setting Boundaries

Setting boundaries is essential for breaking free from busywork. This involves saying no to tasks and commitments that don't align with our goals or values and setting limits on our availability to others. By establishing clear boundaries, we protect our time and energy for the things that truly matter.

Practicing Mindfulness

Practicing mindfulness can also help us break free from busywork. By cultivating present-moment awareness, we become more attuned to our thoughts, feelings, and behaviors. This allows us to recognize when we're engaging in busywork and redirect our attention to more purposeful activities.

Breaking free from busywork is a journey that requires intentionality, self-awareness, and perseverance. By recognizing busywork, prioritizing purposeful work, streamlining processes, setting boundaries, and practicing mindfulness, we can reclaim our time and focus for what truly matters. So, let's embrace the freedom that comes from breaking free from busywork and live more meaningful and fulfilling lives.

Prioritization techniques

These techniques are essential tools for managing our time and resources effectively in today's fast-paced world. With countless tasks vying for our attention, it's easy to feel overwhelmed and unsure of where to focus our efforts. In this chapter, we'll explore various prioritization techniques that can help us make informed decisions about how to allocate our time, energy, and resources.

1. Eisenhower Matrix
The Eisenhower Matrix, also known as the Urgent-Important Matrix, is a powerful tool for prioritizing tasks based on their urgency and importance. It categorizes tasks into four quadrants:

- Quadrant 1: Urgent and Important (Do First) - Tasks that require immediate attention and have a significant impact on our goals or well-being.
- Quadrant 2: Important but Not Urgent (Schedule) - Tasks that are important for our long-term goals but can be scheduled for later.
- Quadrant 3: Urgent but Not Important (Delegate) - Tasks that are urgent but don't contribute to our goals or priorities. These tasks can be delegated to others if possible.
- Quadrant 4: Not Urgent and Not Important (Eliminate) - Tasks that are neither urgent nor important and can be safely eliminated or postponed indefinitely.

By categorizing tasks into these quadrants, we can focus our efforts on the most critical and impactful activities while minimizing distractions and busywork.

2. ABCDE Method

The ABCDE method, popularized by Brian Tracy in his book "Eat That Frog," is another effective prioritization technique. It involves assigning priorities to tasks based on their importance and deadlines:

- A Tasks: High priority tasks with serious consequences if not completed. These tasks should be tackled first.
- B Tasks: Medium priority tasks that contribute to our long-term goals but are not as time-sensitive as A tasks.

- C Tasks: Low priority tasks that can be done if time permits but are not critical to our goals.
- D Tasks: Delegate tasks that can be outsourced to others.
- E Tasks: Eliminate tasks that are not essential and do not contribute to our goals.

By focusing on completing A tasks first and then moving on to B and C tasks, we can ensure that we're making progress on our most important goals while managing our time effectively.

3. The Pareto Principle (80/20 Rule)
The Pareto Principle, also known as the 80/20 rule, states that roughly 80% of results come from 20% of efforts. This principle can be applied to prioritization by identifying the most impactful tasks that yield the greatest results. By focusing our efforts on the 20% of tasks that generate 80% of our desired outcomes, we can maximize our productivity and achieve more with less effort.

4. Time Blocking
Time blocking is a technique that involves scheduling specific blocks of time for different tasks or activities. By allocating dedicated time slots for high-priority tasks, meetings, and breaks, we can ensure that we're using our time efficiently and staying focused on our most important goals. Time blocking also helps prevent

distractions and multitasking by creating dedicated time for focused work.

Prioritization techniques are essential tools for managing our time and resources effectively. By using techniques such as the Eisenhower Matrix, ABCDE method, Pareto Principle, and time blocking, we can make informed decisions about how to allocate our time, energy, and resources to achieve our goals and priorities. So, let's embrace these techniques and take control of our productivity and success.

Chapter 3

The Enemy

Multitasking

In the realm of productivity and efficiency, multitasking often presents itself as a formidable adversary. Despite its perceived allure, multitasking is not the productivity superpower it's often hailed to be. In fact, it's more akin to a deceptive enemy lurking in the shadows, sabotaging our efforts and hindering our ability to perform at our best. Let's delve into why multitasking is considered the enemy of productivity.

The Illusion of Productivity
Multitasking creates the illusion of productivity by allowing us to juggle multiple tasks simultaneously. We might feel like we're accomplishing more in less time, but in reality, our attention is divided, and our performance suffers. Studies have shown that multitasking can lead to a decrease in overall productivity and an increase in errors and inefficiencies.

The Myth of Efficiency
Contrary to popular belief, multitasking does not make us more efficient. When we switch between tasks, our brains need time to refocus and readjust, leading to what psychologists call "switching costs." These switching costs can add up over time, resulting in a significant loss

of productivity. Additionally, multitasking can impair our ability to concentrate and retain information, leading to lower-quality work and increased stress.

The Impact on Quality
One of the most insidious effects of multitasking is its impact on the quality of our work. When our attention is divided among multiple tasks, we're less likely to devote the necessary time and focus to each task, resulting in sloppy work and missed details. This can have serious consequences, particularly in fields where accuracy and attention to detail are paramount.

The Stress Factor
Multitasking also takes a toll on our mental and emotional well-being. Constantly switching between tasks can increase stress levels and lead to feelings of overwhelm and burnout. It creates a sense of mental clutter and chaos, making it difficult to prioritize tasks and stay organized.

The Solution: Single-tasking
To combat the enemy of multitasking, the solution lies in embracing single-tasking - the practice of focusing on one task at a time with full concentration and attention. By dedicating our focus to a single task, we can achieve greater clarity, efficiency, and quality in our work. Single-tasking allows us to fully immerse ourselves in the

task at hand, leading to a deeper level of engagement and satisfaction.

Multitasking may masquerade as a productivity booster, but in reality, it's a stealthy adversary that undermines our performance and well-being. By recognizing the limitations of multitasking and embracing the power of single-tasking, we can overcome this enemy and unlock our full potential for productivity and success.

Distraction

In the battle for productivity and focus, distraction emerges as a formidable adversary. It lurks in the shadows, waiting to pounce on our attention and derail our efforts. Distraction is insidious, constantly vying for our focus and pulling us away from our goals. Let's delve into why distraction is considered the enemy of productivity and how we can combat its influence.

The Fragmentation of Attention
Distraction fragments our attention, dividing it among various stimuli vying for our focus. Whether it's notifications on our smartphones, chatter in the background, or the allure of social media, distractions pull us away from the task at hand, making it difficult to maintain concentration and flow.

The Erosion of Productivity
Distraction erodes our productivity by interrupting our workflow and derailing our momentum. Each distraction pulls us away from our work, requiring time and mental effort to refocus and regain our concentration. These interruptions can add up over time, leading to a significant loss of productivity and a decrease in the quality of our work.

The Toll on Well-being
Distraction takes a toll on our mental and emotional well-being. Constantly switching our attention between tasks and stimuli can increase stress levels and lead to feelings of overwhelm and burnout. It creates a sense of mental clutter and chaos, making it difficult to find peace and focus in our daily lives.

The Cultivation of Mindfulness
To combat the enemy of distraction, we must cultivate mindfulness - the practice of being present and fully engaged in the moment. Mindfulness allows us to become more aware of our thoughts, feelings, and surroundings, helping us recognize when we're being pulled away by distractions and redirect our focus to what truly matters.

The Importance of Boundaries
Setting boundaries is essential for protecting our focus and minimizing distractions. This might involve turning off notifications, creating designated times for checking email and social media, or establishing quiet zones for focused work. By creating a conducive environment for concentration, we can reduce the impact of distractions on our productivity and well-being.

The Power of Focused Work
Focused Work involve immersing ourselves in focused, undisturbed work for extended periods. By eliminating distractions and devoting our full attention to a single task, we can achieve a state of flow and produce high-quality work more efficiently. Deep work requires discipline and practice, but the rewards in terms of productivity and satisfaction are well worth the effort.

In conclusion, distraction may be a pervasive foe in our modern world, but it's not invincible. By cultivating mindfulness, setting boundaries, and embracing the power of deep work, we can combat distraction's influence and reclaim our focus, productivity, and well-being.

Confusion

In the realm of productivity and clarity, confusion emerges as a formidable adversary. It clouds our judgment, muddles our thoughts, and undermines our ability to make informed decisions. Confusion is insidious, creeping into our minds and sowing seeds of doubt and uncertainty. Let's explore why confusion is considered the enemy of productivity and how we can overcome its influence.

The Paralysis of Analysis
Confusion often manifests as a state of indecision and analysis paralysis. When faced with a multitude of options or information overload, we may struggle to discern the best course of action. This indecision can lead to procrastination and inaction, preventing us from moving forward with our goals and tasks.

The Erosion of Clarity
Confusion erodes our clarity of thought, making it difficult to see the big picture and prioritize our tasks effectively. It clouds our judgment and distorts our perceptions, leading to misinterpretations and misunderstandings. Without a clear understanding of our goals and priorities, we may find ourselves wandering aimlessly and expending energy on tasks that don't align with our objectives.

The Cycle of Overwhelm
Confusion often breeds overwhelm, creating a vicious cycle that perpetuates feelings of stress and anxiety. As confusion mounts, so too does our sense of overwhelm,

making it increasingly challenging to regain our footing and regain control of our thoughts and actions. This overwhelm can paralyze us, preventing us from taking decisive action and making progress towards our goals.

The Clarity of Mind

To combat the enemy of confusion, we must cultivate clarity of mind - the ability to see things as they truly are and make decisions with confidence and conviction. Clarity of mind allows us to cut through the noise and confusion, distilling complex information into clear, actionable insights. It empowers us to trust our instincts and intuition, guiding us towards the most effective course of action.

The Power of Simplification

Simplification is a powerful antidote to confusion. By breaking tasks down into smaller, more manageable steps, we can reduce complexity and overwhelm, making it easier to focus and make progress. Simplification involves clarifying our goals and priorities, eliminating distractions, and streamlining our workflows. By simplifying our approach, we can cut through the confusion and regain clarity of purpose.

The Practice of Reflection

Reflection is another effective strategy for overcoming confusion. By taking time to pause and reflect on our thoughts and experiences, we can gain valuable insights and perspective. Reflection allows us to identify patterns, learn from past mistakes, and course-correct as needed. It fosters self-awareness and mindfulness, helping us navigate uncertainty with grace and resilience.

In conclusion, while confusion may pose a formidable challenge to our productivity and clarity, it is not insurmountable. By cultivating clarity of mind, embracing simplification, and practicing reflection, we can overcome confusion's influence and reclaim our focus, confidence, and sense of purpose.

Part 2
Execute
Taking Action Towards Success

1. Focused Action:
  - Single-tasking is a powerful strategy for deepening focus and maximizing productivity.
  - Deep work strategies enable individuals to achieve a state of flow and produce high-quality work.
  - Overcoming procrastination requires understanding its root causes and implementing effective strategies to overcome it.

2. Time Mastery:
  - Effective time management involves minimizing interruptions and implementing time-blocking techniques to optimize productivity.
- Beating deadline stress requires proactive planning, effective delegation, and realistic goal-setting.

Chapter 4

Focused Action

In the pursuit of productivity and goal attainment, executing with focused action emerges as a pivotal strategy. Focused action transcends mere activity; it embodies intentional, purpose-driven effort directed towards a specific objective. Rather than spreading our energy thin across multiple tasks, focused action compels us to concentrate our efforts on the task at hand with unwavering attention and determination. Let's explore this concept practically, diving into the essence of focused action and its transformative impact.

Imagine you're embarking on a project that requires your undivided attention and dedication. Instead of succumbing to distractions and multitasking, you commit to approaching the task with focused action. You create a conducive environment for concentration, minimizing distractions and setting clear boundaries to safeguard your focus. With a clear goal in mind, you immerse yourself fully in the task, channeling your energy and creativity towards its successful completion.

Focused action involves breaking the task down into manageable steps and prioritizing them based on their importance and urgency. Rather than feeling overwhelmed by the enormity of the project, you tackle each step systematically, moving forward with purpose and clarity. You remain adaptable and responsive to challenges, adjusting your approach as needed while staying true to your overarching goal.

Central to focused action is the cultivation of deep work - a state of intense concentration and flow where distractions fade away, and productivity soars. You harness the power of deep work by eliminating interruptions and immersing yourself fully in the task at hand. With sustained focus and attention, you achieve a level of productivity and creativity that transcends ordinary effort.

Focused action is also about maintaining momentum and consistency in the pursuit of our goals. Rather than succumbing to procrastination or inertia, you commit to taking consistent, meaningful action towards your objectives. You set realistic deadlines and hold yourself accountable for progress, celebrating small victories along the way. Through steady, focused effort, you make significant strides towards your goals, one step at a time.

Moreover, focused action requires a mindset of perseverance and resilience. You recognize that setbacks and obstacles are inevitable on the path to success, but you refuse to be deterred. Instead of allowing setbacks to derail your progress, you view them as opportunities for growth and learning. With determination and grit, you

The Power of Single-Tasking

In a world that celebrates multitasking as a symbol of productivity, the power of single-tasking stands as a counterintuitive yet profoundly effective approach to getting things done. Single-tasking involves focusing all of our attention and energy on one task at a time, rather than spreading ourselves thin across multiple activities. Let's explore the transformative impact of single-tasking and why it's a game-changer in our quest for productivity and fulfillment.

Picture yourself at your desk, facing a daunting to-do list overflowing with tasks clamoring for your attention. Instead of succumbing to the temptation to tackle them all simultaneously, you decide to embrace the power of single-tasking. You choose one task, the most important or time-sensitive one, and commit to giving it your undivided attention.

Single-tasking allows you to fully immerse yourself in the task at hand, entering a state of flow where distractions fade away, and productivity soars. You experience a sense of clarity and focus that eludes you when you attempt to juggle multiple tasks simultaneously. With your attention laser-focused on the task in front of you, you're able to work more efficiently and effectively, producing higher-quality results in less time.

Moreover, single-tasking cultivates a sense of mindfulness and presence in our work. Instead of rushing through tasks mindlessly, we approach them with intentionality and purpose, savoring each moment and fully engaging with the task at hand. This mindful approach not only enhances our productivity but also deepens our connection to our work, leading to greater satisfaction and fulfillment.

Single-tasking also enables us to better manage our cognitive resources and combat decision fatigue. When we attempt to multitask, our brains must constantly switch between tasks, depleting our mental energy and impairing our ability to make decisions effectively. By focusing on one task at a time, we conserve our cognitive resources and make clearer, more informed decisions.

Furthermore, single-tasking allows us to prioritize our well-being and reclaim our time. In a culture that glorifies busyness and constant activity, single-tasking serves as a powerful reminder that it's okay to slow down and focus on what truly matters. By eliminating the pressure to do it all, we free ourselves from the tyranny of the never-ending to-do list and create space for rest, relaxation, and rejuvenation.

Deep work

Deep work strategies are essential for maximizing productivity and achieving a state of focused, uninterrupted concentration. Deep work, a concept popularized by author Cal Newport, refers to the ability to immerse oneself fully in cognitively demanding tasks without distractions. Let's explore some effective strategies for incorporating deep work into our daily lives and harnessing its transformative power.

1. Establishing a Dedicated Workspace: Create a designated workspace that is conducive to deep work. Minimize distractions by removing clutter, turning off notifications, and setting boundaries to protect your focus.

2. Setting Clear Goals: Clarify your objectives and prioritize tasks that require deep work. Set specific, measurable goals to guide your efforts and ensure that your deep work sessions are aligned with your long-term objectives.

3. Time Blocking: Allocate dedicated blocks of time for deep work sessions in your schedule. Choose times when you're most alert and focused, and commit to protecting these blocks of time from interruptions and distractions.

4. Implementing Rituals: Develop pre-work rituals to signal to your brain that it's time to enter a state of deep

work. This could involve activities such as meditation, journaling, or listening to instrumental music to help you transition into a focused mindset.

5. Embracing Monotasking: Resist the urge to multitask and focus on one task at a time during deep work sessions. By giving your full attention to the task at hand, you can achieve greater efficiency and produce higher-quality results.

6. Using Time Management Techniques: Experiment with time management techniques such as the Pomodoro Technique or the 90-Minute Focus Session to structure your deep work sessions and maintain productivity throughout.

7. Eliminating Distractions: Identify and eliminate sources of distraction in your environment, whether it's email notifications, social media alerts, or noisy surroundings. Consider using tools such as website blockers or noise-canceling headphones to maintain focus.

8. Practicing Mindfulness: Cultivate mindfulness during deep work sessions by staying present and fully engaged in the task at hand. Notice when your mind starts to wander and gently bring your focus back to the task without judgment.

9. Taking Breaks: Incorporate regular breaks into your deep work schedule to rest and recharge. Use break times to stretch, hydrate, or engage in activities that promote relaxation and mental clarity.

10. Reflecting on Progress: Take time to reflect on your deep work sessions and evaluate your progress towards your goals. Celebrate achievements and identify areas for improvement to refine your deep work practice over time.

The deep work strategies are invaluable tools for maximizing productivity, enhancing focus, and achieving meaningful results. By incorporating these strategies into your routine and cultivating a habit of deep work, you can unlock your full potential and thrive in an increasingly distracted world.

Overcoming Procrastination

Overcoming procrastination is a common challenge that many of us face in our personal and professional lives. Procrastination can manifest in various forms, from delaying important tasks to avoiding difficult decisions. However, with the right strategies and mindset shifts, it's possible to overcome procrastination and achieve greater productivity and fulfillment. Let's explore some effective strategies for overcoming procrastination:

1. Understand the Root Causes: Procrastination often stems from underlying reasons such as fear of failure, perfectionism, or lack of motivation. Take some time to reflect on why you're procrastinating and identify any underlying beliefs or fears that may be holding you back.

2. Break Tasks Down: Large, intimidating tasks can be overwhelming and contribute to procrastination. Break tasks down into smaller, more manageable steps to make them feel less daunting. Focus on completing one small step at a time, gradually building momentum towards your larger goal.

3. Set Clear Goals: Establish clear, specific goals for what you want to accomplish and why it's important to you. Having a clear sense of purpose and direction can help motivate you to take action and overcome procrastination.

4. Use Time Management Techniques: Time management techniques such as the Pomodoro Technique or time blocking can help you structure your time and stay focused on your tasks. Set a timer for a specific period of focused work, followed by a short break, to maintain momentum and productivity.

5. Create a Productive Environment: Designate a dedicated workspace that is free from distractions and conducive to focused work. Turn off notifications,

minimize interruptions, and set boundaries to protect your focus and minimize the temptation to procrastinate.

6. Practice Self-Compassion: Be kind to yourself and practice self-compassion when facing procrastination. Recognize that procrastination is a common struggle and that it's okay to experience setbacks. Instead of dwelling on past mistakes, focus on learning from them and moving forward with renewed determination.

7. Use Implementation Intentions: Implementation intentions involve creating specific plans for when and where you will complete a task. By clearly defining your intentions, you're more likely to follow through and overcome procrastination. For example, instead of saying "I'll work on this project later," say "I'll work on this project for 30 minutes at 2 p.m. in my office."

8. Find Accountability: Share your goals and deadlines with a friend, colleague, or mentor who can hold you accountable and provide support. Having someone to check in with can help keep you motivated and on track, even when you're tempted to procrastinate.

9. Practice Mindfulness: Cultivate mindfulness and present-moment awareness to overcome procrastination. Notice when you're experiencing resistance or procrastinating, and gently redirect your

focus back to the task at hand. Use mindfulness techniques such as deep breathing or meditation to calm your mind and reduce stress.

10. Celebrate Progress: Celebrate your progress and accomplishments, no matter how small. Recognize the effort and determination it takes to overcome procrastination and acknowledge yourself for taking steps towards your goals.

Overcoming procrastination requires a combination of self-awareness, effective strategies, and perseverance. By understanding the root causes of procrastination, setting clear goals, using time management techniques, creating a productive environment, practicing self-compassion, using implementation intentions, finding accountability, practicing mindfulness, and celebrating progress, you can overcome procrastination and unlock your full potential. Remember that overcoming procrastination is a journey, and it's okay to seek support and guidance along the way.

Creating Simple Routines

Creating simple routines is a powerful strategy for enhancing productivity, reducing stress, and cultivating a sense of structure and balance in our lives. Routines provide a framework for organizing our time and activities, making it easier to prioritize tasks, minimize decision fatigue, and maintain consistency in our habits. Let's explore the process of creating simple routines and the benefits they offer:

1. Start with a Clear Vision: Begin by clarifying your goals and priorities. What do you hope to achieve by establishing routines? Whether it's improving productivity, maintaining a healthy lifestyle, or enhancing work-life balance, having a clear vision will guide your routine-building process.

2. Identify Key Areas: Next, identify the key areas of your life that could benefit from routine. This could include morning and evening routines, work routines, exercise routines, meal planning, and leisure activities. Consider where you tend to feel the most stress or disorganization, and prioritize those areas for routine development.

3. Keep It Simple: The key to successful routines is simplicity. Start small and focus on establishing basic, achievable habits that align with your goals. Avoid overcomplicating your routines with unnecessary tasks or unrealistic expectations. The simpler your routines are, the more likely you are to stick with them over the long term.

4. Establish Consistency: Consistency is essential for making routines effective. Choose specific times of day to perform routine activities and stick to them as much as

possible. Consistency helps build momentum and reinforces habits, making them easier to maintain over time.

5. Build in Flexibility: While consistency is important, it's also essential to build flexibility into your routines. Life is unpredictable, and there will inevitably be days when your routine gets disrupted. Instead of abandoning your routine altogether, be prepared to adapt and make adjustments as needed.

6. Prioritize Self-Care: Make self-care a priority in your routines. Incorporate activities that promote physical, mental, and emotional well-being, such as exercise, meditation, journaling, or spending time outdoors. Taking care of yourself is essential for maintaining balance and resilience in the face of life's challenges.

7. Experiment and Iterate: Creating routines is a process of trial and error. Don't be afraid to experiment with different approaches and make adjustments based on what works best for you. Pay attention to how you feel when following your routines and be willing to iterate and refine them over time.

8. Set Realistic Expectations: Be realistic about what you can achieve with your routines. Don't expect overnight success or perfection. Instead, focus on making gradual progress and celebrating small victories along the way.

Remember that consistency and persistence are key to long-term success.

9. Monitor Your Progress: Keep track of your progress and reflect on how your routines are impacting your life. Are you feeling more organized, productive, and balanced? Are there areas where you could make improvements? Regularly evaluating your routines allows you to make informed decisions about how to optimize them for greater effectiveness.

10. Stay Motivated: Finally, stay motivated and committed to your routines by reminding yourself of the benefits they bring. Celebrate your achievements, seek support from friends or family, and find inspiration from others who have successfully implemented routines in their lives. Remember that creating simple routines is a journey, and every step forward brings you closer to your goals.

Creating simple routines is a powerful way to bring structure and balance to our lives. By starting with a clear vision, identifying key areas, keeping it simple, establishing consistency, building in flexibility, prioritizing self-care, experimenting and iterating, setting realistic expectations, monitoring progress, and staying motivated, you can create routines that support your goals and enhance your overall well-being.

Prioritizing Essential Tasks

Prioritizing essential tasks is a fundamental skill for effective time management and productivity. In our fast-paced world filled with numerous demands and distractions, knowing how to identify and prioritize tasks that are essential to our goals and well-being is essential for success. Let's explore this concept extensively:

At its core, prioritizing essential tasks involves distinguishing between what is important and what is urgent. Not all tasks are created equal, and not all tasks deserve our immediate attention. Instead, we must focus on tasks that align with our overarching goals, values, and priorities.

To prioritize essential tasks effectively, it's essential to have a clear understanding of our goals and objectives. What are we working towards? What outcomes are we striving to achieve? By clarifying our goals, we can better assess which tasks are essential for moving us closer to our desired outcomes.

Moreover, prioritizing essential tasks requires discernment and critical thinking. It involves evaluating each task based on its importance, urgency, and impact on our goals. Tasks that contribute directly to our long-term objectives should be prioritized over those that are merely urgent or superficially important.

One effective strategy for prioritizing essential tasks is the Eisenhower Matrix, also known as the Urgent-Important Matrix. This framework categorizes tasks into four quadrants based on their urgency and importance:

- Quadrant 1: Urgent and Important (Do First) - Tasks that require immediate attention and have a significant impact on our goals or well-being.
- Quadrant 2: Important but Not Urgent (Schedule) - Tasks that are important for our long-term goals but can be scheduled for later.
- Quadrant 3: Urgent but Not Important (Delegate) - Tasks that are urgent but don't contribute to our goals or priorities. These tasks can be delegated to others if possible.
- Quadrant 4: Not Urgent and Not Important (Eliminate) - Tasks that are neither urgent nor important and can be safely eliminated or postponed indefinitely.

By categorizing tasks into these quadrants, we can prioritize our efforts and focus on tasks that have the greatest impact on our goals and well-being.

In addition to using frameworks like the Eisenhower Matrix, it's important to consider our personal strengths, preferences, and energy levels when prioritizing tasks. Some tasks may require more mental energy or creative thinking, while others may be more routine or administrative in nature. By aligning tasks with our natural rhythms and preferences, we can maximize our efficiency and effectiveness.

Prioritizing essential tasks also involves being adaptable and responsive to changing circumstances. Flexibility is key, as unexpected challenges or opportunities may arise that require us to adjust our priorities on the fly. By staying agile and open-minded, we can ensure that we're always focusing on what truly matters most.

Ultimately, prioritizing essential tasks is about making intentional choices about how we invest our time and energy. It's about saying no to distractions and non-essential tasks so that we can say yes to our most important priorities. By mastering the art of prioritization, we can achieve greater focus, productivity, and fulfillment in all areas of our lives.

Streamlining Decision-Making

Streamlining decision-making is a crucial skill in today's fast-paced world, where we are bombarded with countless choices and distractions on a daily basis. Making decisions can be mentally taxing and time-consuming, leading to decision fatigue and a sense of overwhelm. However, by implementing strategies to streamline our decision-making process, we can reduce stress, increase efficiency, and make better choices. Let's explore this concept extensively:

Understanding Decision-Making:
Decision-making involves evaluating options and choosing a course of action based on our goals, preferences, and available information. It's a cognitive process that can vary in complexity depending on the context and stakes involved. From simple choices like what to eat for breakfast to more significant decisions like choosing a career path, we make decisions every day that shape our lives.

Challenges of Decision-Making:
While decision-making is an essential aspect of daily life, it can also be fraught with challenges. Decision fatigue, information overload, and analysis paralysis are common obstacles that can hinder our ability to make clear, confident choices. Additionally, emotions, biases, and external pressures can influence our decision-making process, leading to suboptimal outcomes.

Strategies for Streamlining Decision-Making:
1. Clarify Your Priorities: Start by clarifying your goals, values, and priorities. Knowing what matters most to you will help guide your decision-making process and filter out options that don't align with your objectives.

2. Set Decision Criteria: Establish clear criteria for evaluating options and making decisions. Consider factors such as feasibility, impact, cost, and alignment with your goals. Having predefined criteria can simplify

the decision-making process and provide a framework for assessing choices objectively.

3. Limit Options: Too many choices can lead to decision paralysis. Narrow down your options to a manageable number to avoid feeling overwhelmed. Focus on quality over quantity and eliminate choices that don't meet your criteria or are unlikely to lead to a desirable outcome.

4. Use Decision-Making Tools: There are various decision-making tools and techniques available to help streamline the process. For example, decision matrices, pros and cons lists, and weighted decision criteria can provide structure and clarity when evaluating options.

5. Trust Your Intuition: While it's essential to consider relevant information and weigh the pros and cons of each option, sometimes our intuition can provide valuable insights. Pay attention to your gut feelings and instincts, especially when faced with difficult decisions.

6. Avoid Perfectionism: Striving for perfection can paralyze decision-making and lead to unnecessary stress. Recognize that most decisions don't require exhaustive analysis or a perfect solution. Aim for good enough and be willing to accept imperfect outcomes.

7. Set Time Limits: Give yourself a specific time frame for making decisions to avoid prolonged deliberation. Set

deadlines and stick to them to prevent decision procrastination and ensure timely action.

8. Learn from Experience: Reflect on past decisions and their outcomes to learn from experience. What worked well? What could have been done differently? Use insights gained from past experiences to inform future decision-making and improve your decision-making skills over time.

Benefits of Streamlined Decision-Making:

1. Increased Efficiency: Streamlining decision-making saves time and energy, allowing you to focus on more important tasks and priorities.
2. Reduced Stress: Simplifying the decision-making process reduces stress and anxiety associated with indecision and uncertainty.
3. Improved Confidence: Making decisions more efficiently and confidently enhances self-assurance and empowerment.
4. Better Outcomes: By making decisions more systematically and objectively, you're more likely to achieve favorable outcomes and avoid regrets.

Chapter 5

Time Mastery

In the pursuit of productivity and efficiency, mastering our use of time is essential. Yet, in today's fast-paced world, interruptions can disrupt our focus and derail our plans. To reclaim control over our time and optimize our productivity, we must understand the nature of interruptions and implement effective time-blocking techniques. Let's delve into these topics to harness the power of time mastery:

Understanding Interruptions
Interruptions come in various forms, ranging from unexpected phone calls and emails to colleagues dropping by for a quick chat. While some interruptions may be unavoidable, others can be managed effectively with the right strategies. Recognizing the impact of interruptions on our productivity is the first step towards regaining control over our time.

Strategies for Managing Interruptions:

1. Identify Common Sources: Start by identifying common sources of interruptions in your daily routine. Is it frequent email notifications, phone calls, or spontaneous meetings? By pinpointing the most

significant sources of interruptions, you can develop targeted strategies for managing them.

2. Create a Distraction-Free Environment: Designate a distraction-free workspace where you can focus on your tasks without interruptions. Minimize noise, clutter, and visual distractions to create an environment conducive to deep work and concentration.

3. Practice Assertiveness: Learn to assertively communicate your need for uninterrupted focus to colleagues and coworkers. Politely but firmly decline non-urgent requests for your time and attention, and set expectations for when you'll be available to respond.

Time Blocking

Time blocking is a powerful time management technique that involves scheduling specific blocks of time for different tasks and activities. By allocating dedicated time blocks for focused work, meetings, breaks, and personal activities, you can enhance productivity and ensure that your time is used efficiently.

Effective Time Blocking Techniques:
1. Plan Your Day in Advance: Start each day by planning your schedule and allocating time blocks for various tasks and activities. Consider your priorities, deadlines,

and energy levels when structuring your day, and be realistic about how much time each task will require.

2. Use a Calendar or Planner: Use a digital calendar, planner, or time-blocking app to visually organize your schedule and track your time blocks. Color-code different types of activities to distinguish between work-related tasks, personal commitments, and leisure time.

3. Block Off Focus Time: Allocate dedicated time blocks for focused work and deep work sessions. Minimize distractions during these periods by turning off notifications, silencing your phone, and closing unnecessary tabs or windows.

4. Include Buffer Time: Schedule buffer time between time blocks to allow for transitions, breaks, and unexpected delays. Buffer time helps prevent schedule overruns and provides flexibility for handling unforeseen interruptions or emergencies.

5. Review and Adjust Regularly: Regularly review your time-blocking schedule to ensure that it aligns with your priorities and goals. Adjust your schedule as needed based on changes in workload, deadlines, or personal commitments.

Benefits of Time Mastery:
- Increased Productivity: By minimizing interruptions and using time-blocking techniques effectively, you can maximize your productivity and accomplish more in less time.
- Improved Focus and Concentration: Creating a distraction-free environment and allocating focused work time allows you to concentrate deeply on tasks and achieve a state of flow.
- Better Work-Life Balance: Time mastery enables you to prioritize your time effectively and allocate sufficient time for work, personal activities, and leisure pursuits, leading to greater balance and fulfillment.
- Reduced Stress: By proactively managing your time and minimizing interruptions, you can reduce stress and overwhelm associated with deadline pressure and competing demands.

Mastering interruptions and implementing time-blocking techniques are essential steps towards achieving time mastery. By identifying common sources of interruptions, setting boundaries, creating a distraction-free environment, and using time-blocking effectively, you can reclaim control over your time and optimize your productivity. Embrace these strategies to unlock your full potential and achieve greater success and satisfaction in all areas of your life.

Efficient Meetings and Communication

Efficient meetings and communication are crucial components of effective collaboration and productivity in any organization. They serve as the backbone of teamwork, decision-making, and information sharing, facilitating the achievement of common goals and objectives. Let's explore the principles and strategies that underpin efficient meetings and communication:

Clear Objectives: Efficient meetings begin with clearly defined objectives and agendas. Before scheduling a meeting, it's essential to determine the purpose, desired outcomes, and topics to be discussed. Communicate these objectives to participants in advance to ensure alignment and focus.

Streamlined Structure: To avoid wasting time and keep meetings on track, establish a streamlined structure with a clear agenda and timeline. Allocate specific time slots for each agenda item, and stick to the schedule to respect participants' time and maximize productivity.

Engagement and Participation: Encourage active participation and engagement from all meeting attendees to foster collaboration and generate valuable insights. Create a supportive environment where everyone feels comfortable sharing ideas, asking questions, and contributing to discussions.

Effective Facilitation: A skilled meeting facilitator plays a critical role in ensuring that meetings run smoothly and achieve their objectives. The facilitator should guide the discussion, manage time effectively, and facilitate decision-making processes while promoting inclusivity and respect for diverse perspectives.

Use of Technology: Leverage technology to enhance communication and collaboration in meetings. Tools such as video conferencing platforms, collaborative document editing software, and project management tools can facilitate remote meetings, document sharing, and real-time collaboration among team members.

Clear Communication Channels: Establish clear communication channels and protocols to facilitate efficient information sharing and decision-making. Define how information will be disseminated, who is responsible for communication, and how feedback will be collected and addressed.

Feedback Mechanisms: Encourage open and honest feedback from meeting participants to continuously improve communication and collaboration processes. Solicit feedback on meeting effectiveness, communication channels, and decision-making practices to identify areas for improvement and implement corrective actions.

Documentation and Follow-Up: Document key decisions, action items, and next steps during meetings to ensure accountability and follow-through. Distribute meeting minutes or summaries promptly after the meeting to reinforce key takeaways and ensure that everyone is on the same page.

Continuous Improvement: Adopt a mindset of continuous improvement in meetings and communication practices. Regularly evaluate meeting effectiveness, solicit feedback from participants, and implement adjustments to optimize efficiency and effectiveness over time.

Efficient meetings and communication are essential drivers of productivity, teamwork, and organizational success. By adopting clear objectives, streamlined structures, active engagement, effective facilitation, technology integration, clear communication channels, feedback mechanisms, documentation, and a commitment to continuous improvement, organizations can enhance collaboration, decision-making, and overall performance. Embrace these principles and strategies to cultivate a culture of efficiency and excellence in meetings and communication within your organization.

Beating Deadline Stress

We've all been there — staring down the barrel of a looming deadline, feeling the pressure mounting with each passing hour. Whether it's a work project, a school assignment, or a personal goal, deadlines have a way of sneaking up on us and triggering a cascade of stress and anxiety. But fear not, because beating deadline stress is not only possible but entirely within your grasp.

Picture this: you've got a major project due in a week, and it feels like there's a mountain of work standing between you and the finish line. The temptation to procrastinate or panic may be overwhelming, but take a deep breath and remember: you've got this.

The first step in beating deadline stress is to break the task down into smaller, more manageable chunks. Instead of fixating on the enormity of the project as a whole, focus on tackling one step at a time. Set realistic goals for each day or even each hour, and celebrate your progress along the way.

Next, prioritize your tasks based on their importance and urgency. Not all tasks are created equal, so focus your energy on the ones that will have the greatest impact on meeting your deadline. Remember, it's okay to delegate or postpone non-essential tasks if necessary.

Another key strategy for beating deadline stress is to create a realistic timeline for completing the project. Be honest with yourself about how much time you'll need to devote to each task, and build in some buffer room for unexpected setbacks or delays.

Of course, no plan is foolproof, and there may come a time when you hit a roadblock or encounter an unforeseen challenge. When this happens, resist the urge to panic or give up. Instead, take a step back, reassess your approach, and brainstorm alternative solutions. Remember, every setback is an opportunity to learn and grow.

Finally, don't forget to take care of yourself along the way. It's easy to get so caught up in meeting deadlines that we neglect our physical and emotional well-being. Make sure to carve out time for rest, relaxation, and self-care, even in the midst of a busy schedule. A well-rested mind and body are better equipped to handle stress and perform at their best.

So, the next time you find yourself staring down a deadline, remember these simple strategies for beating deadline stress. Break the task down, prioritize your tasks, create a realistic timeline, stay flexible in the face of challenges, and above all, take care of yourself. With a little planning and perseverance, you'll not only meet your deadlines but do so with grace and confidence.

Collaboration and Delegation

Collaboration and delegation are two essential skills for achieving success in both professional and personal endeavors. In today's interconnected world, the ability to work effectively with others and delegate tasks strategically can significantly enhance productivity, innovation, and overall outcomes. Let's explore these concepts and their importance in more detail:

Collaboration
Collaboration involves working together with others to achieve a common goal or objective. It encompasses communication, cooperation, and shared decision-making among team members. Whether it's a small project team, a department within an organization, or a cross-functional team spanning different departments or disciplines, collaboration is essential for harnessing diverse perspectives, skills, and experiences to drive success.

Benefits of Collaboration
1. Increased Creativity and Innovation: Collaboration encourages the exchange of ideas and perspectives, sparking creativity and innovation. By working together, team members can generate new solutions and approaches that may not have been possible working in isolation.

2. Enhanced Problem-Solving: Collaborative teams are better equipped to tackle complex problems and challenges by pooling their collective knowledge and expertise. Different team members may offer unique insights or alternative approaches to problem-solving, leading to more robust solutions.

3. Improved Communication: Collaboration fosters open communication and transparency among team members, leading to clearer expectations, better understanding, and stronger relationships. Effective communication is essential for building trust, resolving conflicts, and maintaining alignment towards common goals.

4. Increased Productivity: When individuals work together towards a common goal, tasks can be divided and conquered more efficiently, leading to increased productivity. Collaboration enables teams to leverage each other's strengths and resources to achieve collective success.

5. Sense of Ownership and Accountability: Collaborative teams often have a greater sense of ownership and accountability for the outcomes of their work. When team members feel invested in the success of the project, they are more likely to take ownership of their responsibilities and strive for excellence.

Delegation

Delegation involves assigning tasks or responsibilities to others who have the necessary skills, knowledge, and authority to carry them out. Effective delegation is not about simply offloading work onto others but rather empowering team members to take ownership and contribute meaningfully to the success of the project or organization.

Benefits of Delegation

1. Improved Time Management: Delegating tasks allows leaders and managers to focus their time and energy on high-priority activities that require their expertise and attention. By redistributing workload strategically, individuals can optimize their time and productivity.

2. Development of Skills and Talent: Delegation provides opportunities for individuals to develop new skills, gain experience, and expand their capabilities. By entrusting tasks to others, leaders can nurture talent within their team and foster professional growth and development.

3. Enhanced Efficiency: Delegating tasks to those best equipped to handle them can streamline processes and increase efficiency. Delegation allows work to be completed more quickly and effectively by leveraging the strengths and expertise of team members.

4. Empowerment and Motivation: Delegating tasks empowers team members to take on new challenges, make decisions, and contribute to the success of the team or organization. When individuals are trusted with responsibility and autonomy, they are more likely to feel motivated and engaged in their work.

5. Reduction of Bottlenecks and Burnout: Delegation helps prevent bottlenecks and burnout by distributing workload evenly among team members. By avoiding overloading individuals with too many responsibilities, delegation promotes a healthier work-life balance and reduces the risk of burnout.

Delegating tasks without micromanaging is a delicate balance that requires trust, clear communication, and empowerment. As a leader or manager, it's essential to empower your team members to take ownership of their responsibilities while providing support and guidance when needed. Let's explore some strategies for delegating tasks effectively without micromanaging:

1. Clearly Define Expectations:
Begin by clearly defining the task or project, including its objectives, scope, and desired outcomes. Provide detailed instructions and guidelines to ensure that the delegated task is understood clearly by the team member. Clarify any questions or concerns upfront to avoid misunderstandings later on.

2. Assign Ownership and Responsibility:

Empower the team member by assigning ownership and responsibility for the delegated task. Make it clear that you trust their abilities and judgment to carry out the task effectively. Encourage them to take initiative, make decisions, and problem-solve independently while keeping you informed of progress along the way.

3. Provide Necessary Resources and Support:

Ensure that the team member has access to the resources, information, and support they need to succeed in completing the delegated task. This may include providing training, tools, or access to relevant documentation or subject matter experts. Offer your assistance and guidance as needed, but avoid overstepping and taking over the task.

4. Set Clear Milestones and Checkpoints:

Establish clear milestones and checkpoints to track progress and ensure that the delegated task stays on track. Break down the task into smaller, manageable steps, and set deadlines for each milestone. Regularly check in with the team member to provide feedback, address any concerns, and offer support as needed.

5. Encourage Open Communication:

Create an environment of open communication where team members feel comfortable asking questions, seeking clarification, and sharing updates on their progress. Encourage two-way communication by actively listening to their input and ideas, and providing constructive feedback and guidance when necessary.

6. Focus on Results, Not Methods:

Focus on the desired results and outcomes of the delegated task, rather than dictating how it should be done. Trust that the team member will approach the task in their own way and allow them the freedom to use their creativity and problem-solving skills. Avoid micromanaging by resisting the urge to control every aspect of the process.

7. Provide Recognition and Feedback:

Acknowledge and recognize the efforts and achievements of the team member as they work on the delegated task. Offer positive reinforcement and praise for their hard work, initiative, and contributions. Provide constructive feedback and guidance to help them improve and grow in their role.

8. Trust and Empower:

Above all, trust your team members to fulfill their responsibilities and make decisions autonomously. Empower them to take ownership of their work and contribute to the success of the team. By demonstrating trust and confidence in their abilities, you'll foster a culture of accountability, empowerment, and mutual respect within your team.

In conclusion, delegating tasks without micromanaging requires a balance of trust, clear communication, and empowerment. By clearly defining expectations, assigning ownership and responsibility, providing necessary support, setting clear milestones, encouraging open communication, focusing on results, providing recognition and feedback, and trusting and empowering your team members, you can delegate tasks effectively while allowing them the autonomy to succeed on their own terms.

Part 3
Thrive
Flourishing in Productive Habits

1. Productive Habits:
- Cultivating consistency in daily routines and habits lays the foundation for sustainable productivity.
- Tracking progress provides valuable feedback and motivation for continued improvement.

2. Work-Life Harmony:
- Building effective teams leverages collective strengths and fosters a culture of collaboration and achievement.

3. Self-Care for High Performers:
- Physical health essentials, such as nutrition, exercise, and sleep, provide the foundation for peak performance.
- Mental resilience enables individuals to navigate challenges with grace and bounce back from setbacks stronger than before.
- Reflecting on milestones allows individuals to acknowledge and appreciate their progress and growth.

Chapter 6

Living the Productive Habits

In this final part of our journey towards productivity and fulfillment, we delve into the essence of thriving – not just surviving, but thriving in every aspect of our lives. It's about embodying the productive habits we've cultivated and integrating them into our daily routines to achieve lasting success and well-being. Let's explore how we can live these productive habits and thrive in all areas of our lives:

1. Cultivate Mindfulness and Presence:
Thriving begins with being fully present in the moment and cultivating mindfulness in our daily lives. Practice mindfulness techniques such as meditation, deep breathing, or mindful movement to center yourself and bring awareness to the present moment. By cultivating mindfulness, you can reduce stress, enhance focus, and cultivate a deeper sense of peace and well-being.

2. Practice Gratitude and Positivity:
Foster an attitude of gratitude and positivity by acknowledging and appreciating the blessings in your life. Take time each day to reflect on the things you're grateful for, no matter how small. By focusing on the positive aspects of your life, you can cultivate a more

optimistic outlook and attract more abundance and joy into your life.

3. Embrace Growth and Learning:
Thriving requires a commitment to lifelong growth and learning. Embrace opportunities for personal and professional development, whether it's through formal education, skill-building workshops, or self-directed learning. Be open to new experiences, challenges, and perspectives, and approach every obstacle as an opportunity for growth.

4. Foster Meaningful Connections:
Invest in nurturing meaningful connections with others – whether it's with family, friends, colleagues, or your community. Prioritize quality time with loved ones, engage in meaningful conversations, and offer support and kindness to those around you. Cultivating strong social connections is essential for fostering a sense of belonging, purpose, and fulfillment.

5. Set Goals and Take Action:
Set clear, achievable goals that align with your values, passions, and aspirations. Break down your goals into actionable steps and create a plan for achieving them. Take consistent, intentional action towards your goals, staying flexible and adaptable in the face of challenges. Celebrate your progress and milestones along the way, and adjust your course as needed to stay on track.

6. Embrace Resilience and Adaptability:

Life is full of ups and downs, challenges, and setbacks. Embrace resilience and adaptability as essential tools for thriving in the face of adversity. Cultivate a growth mindset that sees every obstacle as an opportunity for learning and growth. Develop coping strategies, self-regulation skills, and a strong support network to navigate life's inevitable challenges with grace and resilience.

7. Live with Purpose and Meaning:
Ultimately, thriving is about living with purpose and meaning – aligning your actions with your values, passions, and sense of purpose. Take time to reflect on what matters most to you and what brings you a sense of fulfillment and joy. Live authentically, pursue your passions wholeheartedly, and make a positive impact in the world around you.

Thriving is not just about achieving external success or meeting goals; it's about living with intention, purpose, and fulfillment in every aspect of our lives. By cultivating mindfulness, practicing gratitude, embracing growth, prioritizing self-care, fostering meaningful connections, setting goals, embracing resilience, and living with purpose, we can truly thrive and create a life of abundance, joy, and fulfillment. Embrace these productive habits, integrate them into your daily routines, and watch as you flourish and thrive in all areas of your life.

Cultivating consistency

Cultivating consistency is a powerful practice that lays the foundation for success in all areas of life. It involves committing to regular, deliberate action over time, regardless of external circumstances or obstacles. Consistency is the key to building habits, achieving goals, and realizing long-term growth and fulfillment. Let's explore the concept of cultivating consistency in depth:

Consistency is about showing up day in and day out, even when motivation wanes or challenges arise. It's about making a conscious decision to honor your commitments and follow through on your intentions, no matter what. Consistent action breeds momentum, creating a positive feedback loop that propels you closer to your goals with each step forward.

One of the most significant benefits of cultivating consistency is the development of habits. Habits are formed through repeated actions over time, and consistency is the driving force behind their establishment. By consistently practicing desired behaviors, whether it's exercising regularly, eating healthily, or practicing mindfulness, you can rewire your brain and make these behaviors automatic and effortless.

Consistency also builds trust – trust in yourself and trust from others. When you consistently follow through on your commitments, you demonstrate reliability, integrity, and self-discipline. This builds self-confidence and self-efficacy, as you prove to yourself that you have the power to create positive change in your life. Moreover, others will come to trust and respect you as they witness your consistent actions and reliability.

However, cultivating consistency is not always easy. It requires discipline, perseverance, and a willingness to prioritize long-term benefits over short-term gratification. To cultivate consistency, it's essential to set clear goals, establish routines, and create systems that support your desired behaviors. Break down your goals into manageable tasks and commit to taking consistent action towards them each day.

To cultivate consistency, cultivate self-awareness and self-reflection. Understand your motivations, strengths, and weaknesses, and identify any barriers that may be hindering your consistency. Develop strategies to overcome these obstacles and create accountability mechanisms to help you stay on track.

Building momentum

Building momentum is like igniting a spark that gradually grows into a roaring fire, propelling you forward towards your goals with increasing speed and force. It's about harnessing the power of small, consistent actions to create a powerful wave of progress and momentum in your life. Let's explore how to build momentum and leverage its transformative power:

1. Start Small and Take Consistent Action:
Building momentum begins with taking small, consistent actions towards your goals. Break down your goals into manageable tasks and commit to taking daily steps, no matter how small, towards their achievement. Consistency is key — even small actions can build momentum over time.

2. Celebrate Every Win, No Matter How Small:
Celebrate every win, no matter how small, along the way. Acknowledge your progress and accomplishments, and take a moment to celebrate each milestone you reach. Celebrating your wins reinforces positive behavior and motivates you to keep pushing forward.

3. Focus on Progress, Not Perfection:
Shift your focus from perfection to progress. Understand that progress is not always linear — there will be ups and downs along the way. Embrace the process, learn from setbacks, and keep moving forward, one step at a time.

4. Build Habits and Routines:
Create habits and routines that support your goals and help you stay on track. Consistent habits provide structure and momentum, making it easier to maintain momentum over time. Identify keystone habits – small habits that have a ripple effect on other areas of your life – and prioritize them.

5. Stay Flexible and Adapt to Challenges:
Stay flexible and adapt to challenges as they arise. Building momentum doesn't mean ignoring obstacles or setbacks; it means finding ways to overcome them and keep moving forward. Stay resilient in the face of challenges, and use setbacks as opportunities for growth and learning.

6. Surround Yourself with Positive Influences:
Surround yourself with positive influences – people, environments, and resources that support your goals and inspire you to keep going. Seek out mentors, role models, and supportive communities that can provide encouragement, guidance, and accountability along your journey.

7. Visualize Your Success:
Visualize your success and keep your vision front and center. Create a clear mental image of what success looks and feels like for you, and use this vision to fuel your motivation and drive. Visualization can help you stay

focused and inspired, even when faced with challenges or obstacles.

8. Stay Committed and Keep Going:
Above all, stay committed to your goals and keep going, even when the going gets tough. Building momentum requires perseverance, determination, and a willingness to push through obstacles and setbacks. Trust in yourself and your ability to achieve your goals, and keep taking consistent action towards them every day.

Building momentum is a powerful force that can propel you towards your goals and dreams with unstoppable momentum. By starting small, celebrating wins, focusing on progress, building habits, staying flexible, surrounding yourself with positive influences, visualizing success, and staying committed, you can harness the transformative power of momentum to create the life you desire. Embrace the journey, stay resilient, and keep moving forward – the momentum you build will carry you to new heights of success and fulfillment.

Tracking progress

Tracking progress is a fundamental aspect of personal growth and goal achievement. It involves systematically monitoring and evaluating your performance, milestones, and outcomes over time to ensure that you're moving in the right direction. Effective progress tracking provides valuable insights, accountability, and motivation, helping you stay focused and on track towards your goals. Let's explore how to track progress effectively:

1. Set Clear and Measurable Goals:
Start by setting clear, specific, and measurable goals that outline what you want to achieve and by when. Define key performance indicators (KPIs) or metrics that you can use to track your progress and evaluate success. Break down your goals into smaller, actionable steps to make them more manageable and achievable.

2. Choose the Right Tracking Tools:
Select tracking tools and methods that align with your goals and preferences. This could include digital tools such as spreadsheets, apps, or project management software, or analog methods such as journals, calendars, or progress charts. Choose tools that are easy to use, accessible, and provide the level of detail and customization you need.

3. Establish Regular Check-Ins:
Schedule regular check-ins with yourself to review your progress and assess your performance. This could be daily, weekly, monthly, or at other intervals depending on the nature of your goals and the timeframe for achievement. Use these check-ins to reflect on what's

working well, identify areas for improvement, and make any necessary adjustments to your approach.

4. Track Quantitative and Qualitative Data:
Track both quantitative data (such as numbers, metrics, or milestones) and qualitative data (such as observations, reflections, or feedback) to provide a comprehensive view of your progress. Quantitative data provides objective measures of success, while qualitative data offers insights into your experiences, challenges, and lessons learned.

5. Celebrate Milestones and Achievements:
Celebrate your milestones and achievements along the way to acknowledge your progress and stay motivated. Recognize and reward yourself for reaching key milestones or making significant strides towards your goals. Celebrating achievements reinforces positive behavior and encourages continued effort and commitment.

6. Stay Flexible and Adapt:
Stay flexible and adapt your tracking methods and goals as needed based on your progress and changing circumstances. Be open to feedback, insights, and new information that may influence your approach. Adjust your goals, strategies, or timelines as necessary to stay aligned with your evolving priorities and aspirations.

7. Seek Feedback and Accountability:
Seek feedback from others, such as mentors, peers, or trusted advisors, to gain valuable perspectives on your progress and performance. Accountability partners can provide support, encouragement, and constructive feedback to help you stay accountable and motivated. Share your goals and progress openly with others to cultivate a sense of accountability and commitment.

8. Reflect and Learn from Experience:
Take time to reflect on your progress and learn from your experiences, both successes, and setbacks. Analyze what went well, what didn't, and what you can do differently in the future. Use this self-reflection to refine your goals, strategies, and habits, and continue to grow and improve over time.

Chapter 7

Balancing Ambition and Well-Being

In our fast-paced and goal-oriented society, the pursuit of success and achievement often takes precedence over our well-being. However, finding a balance between ambition and well-being is crucial for long-term happiness, fulfillment, and sustainable success. In this chapter, we explore the importance of striking a healthy balance between ambition and well-being and strategies for achieving this balance:

Understanding Ambition
Ambition is the inner drive and desire to achieve goals, pursue dreams, and reach for success. While ambition can be a powerful motivator for growth and achievement, unchecked ambition can lead to burnout, stress, and dissatisfaction. It's essential to cultivate a healthy relationship with ambition, one that inspires and energizes you without sacrificing your well-being.

Prioritizing Well-Being
Well-being encompasses physical, mental, emotional, and spiritual health — it's about feeling good and functioning well in all areas of your life. Prioritizing well-being means making self-care a non-negotiable priority and nurturing your physical, mental, and emotional health. This includes getting enough sleep, eating

nutritious foods, exercising regularly, managing stress, and engaging in activities that bring you joy and fulfillment.

Recognizing the Impact of Imbalance
When ambition takes precedence over well-being, it can lead to negative consequences such as burnout, fatigue, anxiety, and decreased quality of life. Ignoring the signs of imbalance can ultimately undermine your long-term success and happiness. It's essential to recognize the warning signs of imbalance and take proactive steps to restore equilibrium in your life.

Strategies for Balancing Ambition and Well-Being:

1. Set Realistic Goals: Define clear, achievable goals that align with your values, passions, and priorities. Avoid setting overly ambitious or unrealistic goals that may compromise your well-being.

2. Establish Boundaries: Set boundaries to protect your time, energy, and personal space. Learn to say no to activities or commitments that don't align with your priorities or contribute to your well-being.

3. Practice Mindfulness: Cultivate mindfulness and present-moment awareness to stay grounded and centered amidst the demands of ambition. Practice mindfulness meditation, deep breathing, or other

relaxation techniques to reduce stress and enhance well-being.

4. Schedule Self-Care: Make self-care a regular part of your routine by scheduling time for activities that nourish your body, mind, and soul. Whether it's spending time outdoors, practicing yoga, or enjoying a hobby, prioritize activities that replenish your energy and bring you joy.

5. Seek Support: Don't be afraid to ask for help or seek support when needed. Reach out to friends, family, or professional resources for guidance, encouragement, and perspective.

6. Practice Gratitude: Cultivate an attitude of gratitude by focusing on the blessings in your life and expressing appreciation for the people, experiences, and opportunities that bring you joy and fulfillment.

7. Embrace Flexibility: Be flexible and adaptable in your approach to goal pursuit and achievement. Recognize that setbacks and obstacles are a natural part of the journey and be willing to adjust your plans as needed.

8. Reflect Regularly: Take time to reflect on your priorities, values, and goals regularly. Assess whether your actions and choices are aligned with your overall well-being and make adjustments as necessary.

Reflecting on Milestones, Progress and Growth

Reflecting on milestones is a powerful practice that allows us to pause, acknowledge, and celebrate our progress and growth along our journey. In this chapter, we'll explore the importance of reflecting on milestones and how to incorporate this practice into our lives:

1. Recognizing Achievements:
Reflecting on milestones gives us an opportunity to recognize and celebrate our achievements, both big and small. Whether it's reaching a significant goal, overcoming a challenge, or making progress towards a dream, each milestone represents a step forward on our path to success and fulfillment.

2. Cultivating Gratitude:
Reflecting on milestones cultivates gratitude by encouraging us to acknowledge the blessings and opportunities that have contributed to our success. Gratitude is a powerful antidote to stress and negativity, fostering a sense of abundance and contentment in our lives.

3. Building Confidence and Self-Efficacy:
Celebrating milestones boosts our confidence and self-efficacy by affirming our abilities and accomplishments. When we reflect on how far we've come and what we've achieved, we build a strong sense of self-belief and

resilience that empowers us to tackle future challenges with courage and determination.

4. Providing Perspective:
Reflecting on milestones provides perspective by allowing us to see the bigger picture of our journey. It reminds us of the progress we've made, even in the face of setbacks and obstacles, and helps us stay focused on our long-term goals and aspirations.

5. Inspiring Motivation and Momentum:
Celebrating milestones inspires motivation and momentum by fueling our desire to continue growing and striving for excellence. When we acknowledge our progress and achievements, we're inspired to keep pushing forward and pursuing our dreams with passion and purpose.

6. Enhancing Self-Awareness:
Reflecting on milestones enhances self-awareness by encouraging introspection and self-reflection. It prompts us to examine our strengths, weaknesses, values, and priorities, helping us gain deeper insight into ourselves and our aspirations.

7. Reinforcing Positive Habits and Behaviors:
Celebrating milestones reinforces positive habits and behaviors by recognizing the actions and choices that have contributed to our success. It reinforces the

importance of persistence, resilience, and discipline in achieving our goals, motivating us to continue practicing these behaviors in the future.

8. Strengthening Connections:
Reflecting on milestones strengthens connections with others by fostering a sense of community and shared achievement. It provides an opportunity to express gratitude to those who have supported us along the way and to celebrate our successes with friends, family, and colleagues.

Incorporating Milestone Reflection into Your Life:

1. Set Aside Time for Reflection: Schedule regular time for milestone reflection in your calendar, whether it's weekly, monthly, or quarterly. Create a quiet, peaceful environment where you can reflect without distractions.

2. Journaling: Keep a milestone journal where you document your achievements, progress, and reflections. Write about the milestones you've reached, the lessons you've learned, and the growth you've experienced along the way.

3. Gratitude Practice: Cultivate a gratitude practice as part of your milestone reflection process. Take time to express gratitude for the people, opportunities, and experiences that have contributed to your success.

4. Visualization: Use visualization techniques to imagine your future milestones and successes. Visualize yourself achieving your goals and experiencing the feelings of pride, joy, and fulfillment that come with reaching them.

5. Share Your Successes: Share your milestones and successes with others, whether it's with friends, family, or colleagues. Celebrate your achievements together and bask in the support and encouragement of your loved ones.

In conclusion, reflecting on milestones is a powerful practice that enhances gratitude, builds confidence, provides perspective, inspires motivation, enhances self-awareness, reinforces positive habits, and strengthens connections. By incorporating milestone reflection into your life, you can celebrate your progress, acknowledge your growth, and cultivate a deeper sense of fulfillment and purpose along your journey. Embrace this practice as a source of inspiration and empowerment, and watch as it transforms your life in meaningful and profound ways.

Chapter 8

Harnessing Energy for Productivity and Well-Being

Energy is the currency of life – it powers our actions, fuels our ambitions, and sustains our well-being. In this chapter, we explore the importance of harnessing energy for productivity and well-being and strategies for optimizing your energy levels.

Understanding Energy

Energy is the vital force that drives all aspects of human functioning – physical, mental, emotional, and spiritual. It's the fuel that powers our bodies, minds, and souls, enabling us to think, move, feel, and engage with the world around us. Understanding the different dimensions of energy and how they interact is essential for optimizing our overall well-being and productivity.

Types of Energy
1. Physical Energy: Physical energy is the foundation of our vitality and resilience. It's derived from nutrition, exercise, sleep, and other lifestyle factors that support our physical health and well-being. Physical energy affects our strength, stamina, and ability to perform daily activities with ease and efficiency.

2. Mental Energy: Mental energy encompasses our cognitive functioning, focus, and concentration. It's influenced by factors such as mental stimulation, stress management, and cognitive habits. Mental energy impacts our ability to think critically, solve problems, and maintain mental clarity and alertness throughout the day.

3. Emotional Energy: Emotional energy relates to our feelings, emotions, and mood states. It's influenced by factors such as emotional regulation, social connections, and psychological well-being. Emotional energy affects our resilience, motivation, and capacity for empathy, compassion, and emotional intelligence.

4. Spiritual Energy: Spiritual energy pertains to our sense of purpose, meaning, and connection to something greater than ourselves. It's nurtured through practices such as meditation, prayer, reflection, and acts of kindness. Spiritual energy provides a sense of inner peace, fulfillment, and alignment with our deepest values and aspirations.

Optimizing Energy Levels
1. Prioritize Sleep: Prioritize quality sleep to recharge your physical, mental, and emotional energy reserves. Aim for 7-9 hours of uninterrupted sleep each night and establish a consistent sleep schedule to optimize your circadian rhythms.

2. Fuel Your Body: Eat a balanced diet rich in whole foods, fruits, vegetables, lean proteins, and healthy fats to fuel your body with essential nutrients and sustain energy levels throughout the day. Stay hydrated by drinking plenty of water and limit consumption of caffeine and sugary drinks.

3. Move Your Body: Incorporate regular physical activity into your daily routine to boost physical energy, improve mood, and reduce stress. Choose activities you enjoy, whether it's walking, running, yoga, or dancing, and aim for at least 30 minutes of moderate exercise most days of the week.

4. Manage Stress: Practice stress management techniques such as deep breathing, meditation, mindfulness, and progressive muscle relaxation to reduce stress levels and conserve mental and emotional energy. Prioritize self-care activities that promote relaxation and rejuvenation, such as spending time in nature, reading, or practicing hobbies.

5. Cultivate Positive Relationships: Cultivate supportive relationships and social connections that nourish your emotional well-being and provide a sense of belonging and support. Spend time with friends, family, and loved ones who uplift and inspire you, and prioritize quality time together.

6. Set Boundaries: Set boundaries to protect your energy and prevent burnout. Learn to say no to activities, commitments, or relationships that drain your energy or compromise your well-being. Prioritize activities and relationships that align with your values and bring you joy and fulfillment.

7. Practice Self-Reflection: Take time for self-reflection and introspection to assess your energy levels, identify areas of imbalance, and make adjustments as needed. Regularly check in with yourself to gauge your physical, mental, emotional, and spiritual well-being and make self-care a priority.

8. Align with Purpose: Align your actions and goals with your sense of purpose and values to tap into a deeper source of motivation and fulfillment. Cultivate a sense of meaning and connection to something greater than yourself, whether it's through work, hobbies, relationships, or community involvement.

Harnessing energy for productivity and well-being is essential for living a vibrant, fulfilling life. By understanding the different dimensions of energy and how they interact, prioritizing sleep, nutrition, exercise, stress management, social connections, setting boundaries, practicing self-reflection, and aligning with purpose, you can optimize your energy levels and thrive in all aspects of your life. Embrace energy as a precious resource and invest in practices that replenish, recharge, and sustain your vitality and well-being.

Building effective teams

Building effective teams is a cornerstone of success in any organization. A well-functioning team can achieve more than the sum of its individual members, leveraging diverse skills, perspectives, and strengths to drive innovation, problem-solving, and results. In this note, we'll explore the principles and strategies for building effective teams:

1. Clear Vision and Goals:
Establish a clear vision and set of goals that articulate the purpose, mission, and objectives of the team. Ensure that every team member understands and aligns with the vision and goals, providing clarity and direction for collective efforts.

2. Strong Leadership:
Effective teams require strong leadership to guide and support members, foster collaboration, and drive performance. Leaders should inspire trust, provide clear direction, empower team members, and create a culture of accountability and excellence.

3. Diverse Skill Sets and Perspectives:
Assemble a diverse team with a range of skills, experiences, and perspectives that complement one another. Diversity fosters creativity, innovation, and adaptability, enabling teams to tackle complex challenges and opportunities from multiple angles.

4. Clear Roles and Responsibilities:
Define clear roles, responsibilities, and expectations for each team member to ensure accountability and promote collaboration. Clarify who is responsible for what tasks, decisions, and deliverables, minimizing confusion and overlap.

5. Effective Communication:
Communication is the lifeblood of effective teams. Foster open, honest, and transparent communication channels that enable team members to share ideas, provide feedback, and collaborate effectively. Encourage active listening, respect diverse viewpoints, and address conflicts constructively.

6. Trust and Psychological Safety:
Build trust and psychological safety within the team, creating an environment where members feel safe to take risks, express themselves, and challenge the status quo. Trust enables teams to collaborate more effectively, share ideas openly, and navigate conflicts constructively.

7. Collaboration and Teamwork:

Promote collaboration and teamwork as core values within the team. Encourage collective problem-solving, knowledge sharing, and mutual support among team members. Foster a culture of collaboration where individuals feel valued, respected, and empowered to contribute.

8. Continuous Learning and Improvement:

Cultivate a culture of continuous learning and improvement within the team. Encourage experimentation, innovation, and reflection on both successes and failures. Celebrate achievements and milestones, while also using setbacks as opportunities for growth and learning.

9. Flexibility and Adaptability:

Teams must be flexible and adaptable in response to changing circumstances, priorities, and challenges. Embrace agility and resilience, adjusting plans and strategies as needed to stay aligned with goals and respond to emerging opportunities or threats.

10. Recognition and Celebration:

Recognize and celebrate the contributions and achievements of team members regularly. Acknowledge individual efforts, milestones, and successes, reinforcing positive behavior and fostering a sense of pride and camaraderie within the team.

11. Accountability and Performance Management:
Hold team members accountable for their performance,
ensuring that commitments are met and results are
achieved. Establish clear metrics, KPIs, and performance
standards to monitor progress and provide feedback on
individual and team performance.

Nurturing relationships

Nurturing relationships is a fundamental aspect of
human connection and personal growth. It involves
cultivating meaningful connections with others based on
mutual trust, respect, and care. Nurturing relationships
requires time, effort, and emotional investment, but the
rewards – including increased happiness, support, and
fulfillment – are well worth it.

At its core, nurturing relationships is about prioritizing
the well-being and happiness of both yourself and
others. It means showing kindness, compassion, and
empathy towards others, and being willing to listen,
understand, and support them in times of need. It's
about building strong foundations of trust and
communication, and fostering an environment where
individuals feel valued, respected, and accepted for who
they are.

Effective communication is a cornerstone of nurturing
relationships. It involves not only speaking openly and

honestly but also actively listening to others with empathy and understanding. By truly listening to others' thoughts, feelings, and perspectives, we demonstrate that we care and respect their experiences, which strengthens the bonds of trust and connection between us.

Additionally, nurturing relationships requires investing time and effort into maintaining and deepening connections with others. This may involve spending quality time together, sharing experiences, and creating memories that strengthen the bond between individuals. It also means being there for each other during both the good times and the bad, offering support, encouragement, and companionship when needed.

Chapter 9

Self-Care for High Performers

In the fast-paced world of high performance, the pressure to excel can often lead to neglecting one's own well-being. However, self-care is essential for maintaining peak performance and preventing burnout. In this chapter, we'll explore mindfulness practices as a cornerstone of self-care for high performers:

Understanding Mindfulness:
Mindfulness is the practice of being fully present and engaged in the present moment, with an attitude of openness, curiosity, and non-judgment. It involves cultivating awareness of your thoughts, feelings, sensations, and surroundings, without becoming overwhelmed or reactive to them. Mindfulness enables high performers to cultivate mental clarity, emotional resilience, and inner peace amidst the demands of their busy lives.

Benefits of Mindfulness for High Performers:

1. Stress Reduction: Mindfulness has been shown to reduce stress levels by activating the body's relaxation response and promoting a sense of calm and well-being.

2. Improved Focus and Concentration: Regular mindfulness practice enhances focus, attention, and concentration, allowing high performers to stay present and engaged in their tasks without getting distracted.

3. Enhanced Emotional Regulation: Mindfulness helps high performers develop greater emotional intelligence and resilience, enabling them to respond to challenges with clarity, composure, and compassion.

4. Increased Creativity and Innovation: Mindfulness fosters a state of relaxed awareness that enhances creativity, problem-solving, and innovation, enabling high performers to think outside the box and generate fresh ideas.

5. Better Decision-Making: By cultivating mindfulness, high performers can make more informed, thoughtful decisions based on a clear understanding of their values, priorities, and goals.

Mindfulness Practices for High Performers

1. Mindful Breathing: Take a few moments each day to focus on your breath, paying attention to the sensations of inhaling and exhaling. This simple practice can help calm the mind, reduce stress, and promote relaxation.

2. Body Scan Meditation: Practice a body scan meditation, where you systematically scan your body from head to toe, bringing awareness to any areas of tension or discomfort. This practice promotes relaxation and body awareness.

3. Mindful Movement: Engage in mindful movement practices such as yoga, tai chi, or qigong, where you move your body with awareness and intention. These practices not only promote physical health and flexibility but also cultivate mindfulness and presence.

4. Mindful Eating: Practice mindful eating by paying attention to the sensory experience of eating – the colors, textures, flavors, and smells of your food. Eat slowly, savoring each bite, and notice how it nourishes and satisfies your body.

5. Mindful Walking: Take mindful walks in nature, paying attention to the sights, sounds, and sensations around you. Notice the beauty of your surroundings and the rhythm of your footsteps, allowing yourself to be fully present in the moment.

6. Mindful Work Breaks: Take short mindfulness breaks throughout the day to pause, breathe, and recenter yourself. This can be as simple as taking a few deep breaths, stretching your body, or practicing a quick mindfulness meditation

Incorporating Mindfulness into Daily Life
To reap the benefits of mindfulness, it's important to integrate these practices into your daily routine. Start with small, manageable steps, such as setting aside a few minutes each day for mindfulness meditation or incorporating mindfulness into everyday activities like eating, walking, or working. Over time, you can gradually expand and deepen your mindfulness practice, noticing the positive impact it has on your performance, well-being, and overall quality of life.

Physical Health Essentials

Physical health is the foundation of overall well-being and vitality. In this chapter, we'll explore the essential components of physical health and strategies for optimizing them:

1. Nutrition:
A balanced diet rich in nutrients is essential for maintaining optimal physical health. Focus on consuming a variety of whole foods, including fruits, vegetables, lean proteins, whole grains, and healthy fats. Limit processed foods, sugary snacks, and excess sodium and saturated fats. Stay hydrated by drinking plenty of water throughout the day.

2. Exercise:
Regular physical activity is crucial for cardiovascular health, muscular strength, flexibility, and overall fitness. Aim for at least 150 minutes of moderate-intensity exercise or 75 minutes of vigorous-intensity exercise each week, along with muscle-strengthening activities on two or more days per week. Find activities you enjoy, whether it's walking, jogging, swimming, cycling, yoga, or strength training, and incorporate them into your routine.

3. Sleep:
Quality sleep is essential for physical health, cognitive function, and emotional well-being. Aim for 7-9 hours of uninterrupted sleep each night, and establish a consistent sleep schedule by going to bed and waking up at the same time every day. Create a relaxing bedtime routine to signal to your body that it's time to wind down, such as reading, taking a warm bath, or practicing relaxation techniques like deep breathing or meditation.

4. Hygiene:
Maintaining good hygiene practices is essential for preventing illness and promoting overall health. Practice regular handwashing with soap and water, especially before eating, after using the bathroom, and after touching surfaces in public places. Shower regularly, brush your teeth twice a day, floss daily, and schedule

regular check-ups with your healthcare provider for preventive care.

5. Stress Management:
Chronic stress can have a significant impact on physical health, contributing to a wide range of health problems, including heart disease, obesity, and weakened immune function. Practice stress management techniques such as mindfulness meditation, deep breathing, progressive muscle relaxation, yoga, or spending time in nature to reduce stress levels and promote relaxation.

6. Regular Medical Check-ups:
Schedule regular medical check-ups with your healthcare provider for preventive care and early detection of health issues. Stay up to date on vaccinations, screenings, and health assessments recommended for your age, gender, and medical history. Be proactive about addressing any concerns or symptoms you may have, and don't hesitate to seek medical attention if needed.

7. Avoidance of Harmful Substances:
Avoiding harmful substances such as tobacco, alcohol, and recreational drugs is essential for maintaining optimal physical health. Smoking is a leading cause of preventable disease and death worldwide, so if you smoke, seek support to quit. Limit alcohol consumption to moderate levels (up to one drink per day for women

and up to two drinks per day for men) and avoid illicit drugs altogether.

8. Sun Protection:
Protecting your skin from the sun's harmful ultraviolet (UV) rays is crucial for preventing skin cancer and premature aging. Wear sunscreen with a broad-spectrum SPF of 30 or higher, even on cloudy days, and reapply it every two hours or after swimming or sweating. Wear protective clothing, sunglasses, and hats when spending time outdoors, and seek shade during peak sun hours.

In conclusion, prioritizing physical health essentials is essential for maintaining overall well-being and vitality. By focusing on nutrition, exercise, sleep, hygiene, stress management, regular medical check-ups, avoidance of harmful substances, and sun protection, you can optimize your physical health and enjoy a higher quality of life. Embrace these strategies as cornerstones of your self-care routine, and watch as they contribute to your long-term health and happiness.

Thriving in the Face of Challenges

Mental resilience is the ability to bounce back from adversity, cope with stress, and thrive in the face of challenges. In today's fast-paced and unpredictable world, cultivating mental resilience is essential for navigating life's ups and downs with grace and strength.

In this chapter, we'll explore practical strategies for building mental resilience that anyone can apply in their daily lives:

1. Embrace the Growth Mindset:
Developing a growth mindset is essential for building mental resilience. Embrace challenges as opportunities for growth and learning, rather than viewing them as threats or failures. Cultivate a belief in your ability to learn, adapt, and overcome obstacles through effort and perseverance.

2. Practice Self-Compassion:
Be kind to yourself during difficult times and treat yourself with the same compassion and understanding that you would offer to a friend. Acknowledge your feelings without judgment, and remind yourself that it's okay to struggle. Treat yourself with gentleness and kindness, and practice self-care activities that nourish your body, mind, and soul.

3. Develop Coping Skills:
Build a toolbox of coping skills that help you manage stress and navigate challenging situations. This could include deep breathing exercises, mindfulness meditation, journaling, or engaging in hobbies or activities that bring you joy and relaxation. Experiment with different techniques to find what works best for you.

4. Cultivate Social Support:

Lean on your support network during tough times and reach out to friends, family, or trusted mentors for encouragement and guidance. Surround yourself with positive influences who lift you up and offer support when you need it most. Don't be afraid to ask for help or seek professional support if you're struggling to cope on your own.

5. Focus on What You Can Control:

Shift your focus away from things that are beyond your control and instead concentrate on what you can influence. Break challenges down into smaller, manageable steps, and take proactive action to address them. Practice acceptance of the things you cannot change and focus your energy on making positive changes where you can.

6. Find Meaning and Purpose:

Connect with your values, passions, and sense of purpose to find meaning in difficult situations. Reflect on what matters most to you and how you can align your actions with your values. Engage in activities that give your life meaning and purpose, whether it's volunteering, pursuing creative endeavors, or spending time with loved ones.

7. Foster Optimism and Gratitude:
Cultivate a positive outlook on life by focusing on gratitude and cultivating optimism. Keep a gratitude journal where you write down three things you're thankful for each day. Practice reframing negative thoughts into more positive, empowering ones, and look for silver linings in challenging situations.

8. Build Resilient Relationships:
Nurture strong, supportive relationships with others that provide a source of strength and encouragement during tough times. Surround yourself with people who uplift you, offer perspective, and help you see challenges as opportunities for growth. Invest time and energy into building and maintaining these relationships.

In conclusion, building mental resilience is an ongoing process that requires practice, patience, and self-compassion. By embracing challenges as opportunities for growth, practicing self-compassion, developing coping skills, cultivating social support, focusing on what you can control, finding meaning and purpose, fostering optimism and gratitude, and building resilient relationships, you can strengthen your mental resilience and thrive in the face of adversity. Embrace these practical strategies in your daily life, and watch as they empower you to navigate life's challenges with resilience, courage, and grace.

Conclusion

In the journey through "Productivity the Lazy Way: How Smartness Wins Over Long Hours," we've traversed the landscape of productivity, exploring the depths of efficiency, resilience, and fulfillment. Rooted in the philosophy that working smarter, not harder, is the key to sustainable success, this book has offered insights, strategies, and practical tools to help readers thrive in a world that often glorifies hustle over effectiveness.

Throughout the pages of this book, we've challenged conventional wisdom and debunked the myth of endless hustle. We've embraced the art of lazy productivity, recognizing that true efficiency lies not in the quantity of work accomplished, but in the quality and impact of our efforts. By simplifying our approach, prioritizing tasks, and focusing on meaningful action, we've discovered that productivity can be achieved with less stress, less overwhelm, and less burnout.

In Part 1: Simplify, we learned the importance of streamlining our workflows, decluttering our minds, and embracing smart strategies to optimize our productivity. We shifted our mindset from busyness to effectiveness, recognizing that it's not about how much we do, but how well we do it. By prioritizing essential tasks, breaking free from busywork, and eliminating distractions, we've laid the groundwork for lazy productivity to flourish.

Part 2: Execute took us deeper into the realm of action, exploring the power of focused effort, disciplined time management, and resilient mindset. We discovered the potency of single-tasking, deep work, and overcoming procrastination to unlock our full potential. By mastering time, beating deadline stress, and embracing productive habits, we've cultivated a foundation for sustained success and achievement.

In Part 3: Thrive, we shifted our focus from mere productivity to holistic well-being, recognizing that true success encompasses not only professional accomplishments but also personal fulfillment and happiness. We explored the importance of work-life harmony, self-care, and celebrating success as integral components of a fulfilling life. By nurturing relationships, fostering resilience, and finding joy in our accomplishments, we've embraced a holistic approach to productivity that honors our humanity and enriches our lives.

As we conclude this journey, let us remember that productivity is not a destination but a lifelong pursuit. It's about continuously refining our strategies, adapting to change, and aligning our actions with our values and aspirations. Whether we're striving for professional success, personal growth, or simply a more balanced and fulfilling life, the principles of lazy productivity offer a roadmap for achieving our goals with intention, efficiency, and grace.

So, as you close the final chapter of this book, I invite you to reflect on your own journey towards productivity the lazy way. What insights have you gained? What strategies will you implement? And how will you continue to cultivate a life of purpose, passion, and productivity? Remember, the power to create the life you desire lies within you. Embrace the art of lazy productivity, and watch as it transforms your work, your relationships, and your life.